# NORTHAMPTON BUSES

JOHN EVANS

AMBERLEY

First published 2018

Amberley Publishing
The Hill, Stroud
Gloucestershire, GL5 4EP

www.amberley-books.com



ISBN 978 1 4456 7356 1 (print)
ISBN 978 1 4456 7357 8 (ebook)



British Library Cataloguing in Publication Data.
A catalogue record for this book is available from the British Library.

Origination by Amberley Publishing.
Printed in the UK.

# Contents

# Transport for All

Omnibus – from Latin, meaning 'for all'. An appropriate description, perhaps, of one of our most humble and human creations. Born to work, it wakes in the morning when the engine is switched on and slumbers at night, as if taking a well-earned rest. It needs sustenance in the form of fuel and maintenance. It offers none of the pretensions of a long-distance coach, a vehicle which in too many ways is inferior to a train. Buses are practical, peripatetic and unglamorous. They have a clearly defined purpose in life – to move multitudes of people safely, cheaply and in passable comfort over relatively short distances. People of all kinds, from all places – 'for all'. Buses provide an excellent way of viewing our environment ... and of studying our fellow human beings, as we sit there psychoanalysing other passengers. Why is the man in the chalk-striped suit and silk tie using a bus? Is it simply more convenient? Is his car off the road? Has he lost his driving licence through some indiscretion?

When I lived in California, I regularly travelled by bus. In the city of the car, my neighbours simply did not understand it.

Chatting over a beer one night, Jeff summed up his feelings: 'I don't get this bus thing, man. You have a yellow Corvette in your garage and yet you go downtown on a bus.' He examined me with the look of a weary parent attempting to tell a child why fire is dangerous.

'I like buses, Jeff,' I explained. 'They are a slice of life, a microcosm of society in one thirty-foot long tube. Besides, someone else drives and I don't have to park.'

Buses provide adventures. In Barbados I travelled on a rocket ship of a single-decker, the driver racing along like Lewis Hamilton as we swept towards Bridgetown. The vehicle was heaving with conversation and mine was the only white face on board. I loved every minute. In Tafraoute, Morocco, three of us joined a dishevelled old French bus heading for the centre of town to visit a restaurant. We sat down on ripped seats in an ancient and disgusting vehicle reeking of vile-smelling cigarettes as chickens ran up the centre aisle. Nobody collected the fare and we got a free ride. Buses are like that. In Pasadena, California, the buses were spotlessly clean and had free Wi-Fi when it was unheard of elsewhere.

We usually remember our first flight in an aeroplane, but seldom our first bus journey. For my family, one of the delights on a Sunday afternoon in the 1950s was a trip from our home in Northampton to Wellingborough Zoo. The animals were supposed to be the highlight of the visit, but I really preferred the bus ride. This involved boarding a green United Counties double-decker in Wellingborough Road and obviously my brother and I wanted to sit upstairs, front seat. The layout of the Wellingborough bus was completely different from the vermilion Northampton Corporation vehicles that we used when travelling to the centre of town. Upstairs it had a low aisle on the right side and you stepped up to get into the seats, which were in long horizontal rows. This was quite inconvenient, as passengers sitting near the left-hand window had to move everyone to get out of their seat. The peculiar corridor, however, allowed it to pass beneath low bridges. Here was a bus with personality, cleverly designed to adapt to its environment.

This book takes you on a journey, from horse-drawn trams to modern fleets of air-conditioned buses. They all have one thing in common – to move the people of Northampton around. My research made me aware of just how much affection there is towards buses, especially older ones. I met a man who bought a sixty-year-old Northampton bus from a scrapyard and had it rebuilt as new with the help of many talented supporters. I totally understand why.

The town has an interesting transport history and I hope this overview of Northampton's buses will satisfy both general readers and enthusiasts. I must place on record my grateful thanks to those who have helped my research, especially J. P. and his staff at the Discovery Room at Northampton Central Library. My thanks also go to the team at Northampton Record Office; Nick and Jane Evans; Adrian Griffiths; Mike Dean; Philip Watts; Richard Denny; Robert Edwards; Patrick Rawlinson; Bob Mullins; Graham Onley; Nick Spoors at the *Northampton Chronicle & Echo*; and Paul Brookfield. Special thanks must go to John Child, who put his vast collection of Northampton bus photographs and memorabilia at my disposal. Photographs not credited are my own.

John Evans
Luddenden, West Yorkshire
November 2017

Buses, Barbados style; on board a Hino vehicle, racing towards Bridgetown on 21 June 2014.

# Buses, Boots and Shoes

Northampton in the 1950s was a very different place from today. It had the intrinsic qualities of a likeable but unprepossessing county town. Ecclesiastically it lived in the shadow of Peterborough Cathedral, some 45 miles away, and at the far end of a long and sprawling county. It never rated in the list of Britain's most beautiful towns. Northampton was simply a businesslike, workaday place halfway between London and Birmingham. Yet, in terms of footwear manufacturing, it stood in the shadows of nowhere. Shrouded in fascinating history, Northampton (once 'Hamtune', the village by the meadow) had a boot and shoe industry that went back 500 years. The leather-centred Northampton of the late nineteenth century saw its population rise swiftly from 41,000 in 1871 to 61,000 in 1891. About 40 per cent of those people worked in the shoe industry, all travelling daily to work as clickers and cobblers. Into that scenario came the town's first proper public transport – the horse tram – and it wasn't all plain sailing.

We are standing at the top of Abington Street, looking downhill towards the town centre on 20 April 1901. For the past twenty years, the town's population has been served by a network of trams. These are drawn by pairs of horses and offer fairly rudimentary protection for passengers. Upstairs there is a gallery surrounding the seats. The lower deck is enclosed with windows, the whole vehicle being mounted on a four-wheel chassis which offers a fairly jolty ride.

Suddenly, there is a moment of panic. The tram is running away downhill because the brakes have failed. The driver fights to retain control and, as we watch, a man and a child leap off. Others follow. A police officer standing nearby shouts a warning and tries to slow the tram, but it sways, swerves and eventually overturns. The tragedy leads to twenty people being injured, many of whom jumped off. There was one fatality. Later, Harry Pell, the conductor – who lived to be in his nineties – told how the brakes failed completely and he had also leapt off. There was a public collection for one of those involved in the accident. Yet, tramways were seen as essentially safe. The first networks were a natural development of stage coaches, but allowed horses to pull a heavier weight than if they were moving coaches on roads. Smooth and efficient, they soon became a popular form of local transport, and in Northampton, at a time of rapid population growth, a system was created for the town by the Northampton Street Tramways Company with stables off Abington Street. The first route opened on 4 June 1881, serving the Kettering Road, the Racecourse, the Kingsley Park Hotel (later the White Elephant) and Kingsley Park Road. The network expanded over the next twelve years to take in Kingsthorpe, St James, Weston Favell and South Bridge. The route to Weston Favell took in the important Mansfield Shoe Factory in Wellingborough Road, which by then was employing more than 1,000 people. Eight tramcars were used, built by the Birmingham Railway & Carriage Works, with each seating eighteen inside and a similar number outside and being pulled by two horses. Records show they were made of wood and painted green with green velvet seats. However, the new undertaking was in financial trouble only four years after opening, so to save money the tramcars had the upstairs seats removed, allowing them to be pulled by just one horse. They also hired boys to replace adult conductors. This stabilised the company, and by 1893, new lightweight tramcars were being built.

Horse tram No. 15, built by Falcon, is seen here when new in 1893. It was purchased to strengthen the fleet when the Wellingborough Road service was opened. Local dignitaries are posing in the photograph, seen before protective 'decency boards' containing route information were fitted alongside the upper deck. This is the tram that was involved in the Abington Street accident. The tram is at St James' Square, known locally as 'Café Square' to differentiate it from St James' Square near Kingswell Street. (John Child Collection)

# The Heyday of the Tram

The Tramways & Electric Light Committee of the council decided to compulsorily purchase Northampton Street Tramways for £37,500 in October 1901 under a law allowing this. This offer was initially refused by the company, reported the *Northampton Mercury* newspaper, but later a deal was done for an additional £1,200. The same journal advised its readers that the council had inherited 102 horses and twenty-two cars, constituting a system that had carried 2,292,000 passengers. The purchase decision was clearly not controversial – 'every hand was held up in favour', reported the *Mercury*. The new system became known as Northampton Corporation Tramways and tramcar sheds were built at St James' End with a power supply building in Castle Street, north of the town centre.

An ignominious end for an electric tram being transported from St James's along the Weedon Road to a local farm for use as storage in January 1935 following closure of the tram system the previous month. (W. J. S. Meredith)

The end of an era – Far Cotton was, in 1914, the only route still using horse buses. Here is one of the last of them on their final day in service in October 1914. Alderman Francis Stiles is sitting on the upper deck, offside. The scene is outside All Saints' Church. (John Child Collection)

The Drapery in 1904, with cobbled streets and a tram heading north. This is No. 7, which has an open roof. (John Child Collection)

# The End of the Horse Tram

Horse trams, however, were already old technology. The first electric tramway system had opened in Russia even before Northampton's horse trams started work, and in many parts of the world it was clear that electricity was the future. Horses were labour-intensive, dumped their manure on town streets and could work for only a limited duration. In contrast, electric trams were convenient, comfortable and, once the infrastructure had been installed, cheap to run. Plans had been announced to electrify the Northampton system back in 1897 and initially six double-deck trams worked the first electric services, which started in 1904. As horse trams were replaced, the electric network expanded very quickly, with most parts of the town being electrified within a few months. One problem was at Far Cotton, where the London & North Western Railway refused to allow trams over the Bridge Street crossing. It was not until 1914 that an agreement was concluded; before that, passengers had to get off their tram, walk over the crossing and travel using another tram that was hauled by a steam roller.

By 1911 the population of Northampton had reached 90,000, but then growth tailed off. The town bustled with shoe machinery companies as mechanisation became the new buzzword. In contrast to the fairly stable population, however, big changes were taking place in the transport system.

Tram No. 11 is returning to town past the Kingsley Park Hotel, later the White Elephant, in about 1918. Another tram can be glimpsed approaching the terminus at St Matthew's Church, while a London & North Western Railway horse-drawn delivery van is on the left. The man with a bike seems worryingly close to the approaching tram. (John Child Collection)

Car No. 19 is seen here in Mercers Row, with All Saints' Church on the right before the railings were removed and the road widened. It was one of the original trams delivered in 1904, to be later modernised with a roof and different staircase. Trams were the main source of local transportation in the 1920s. (John Child Collection)

St Matthew's Parade in the early 1920s, with No. 25 in action. Much of the elegant scrollwork on the poles carrying the overhead wires was later removed to make painting easier. (John Child Collection)

In 1914 came the first trams with roofs. One of them is seen here just after entering service at Franklins Gardens. They were numbered from 27 to 33 and offered much better protection for both passengers and motormen. (John Child Collection)

Mercers Row in 1932 with enclosed, single-deck tram No. 34 on a St James service. We get an excellent view of Wood Hill. (M. J. O'Connor)

# The Arrival of the Motor Bus

As a Corporation undertaking, the colour of the trams had changed to cream and vermilion – a bright red with more than a touch of orange. This livery was to last, in various forms, to the end of Northampton Corporation Transport's services and is faithfully reproduced today on preserved Northampton Corporation buses. After coping with the First World War, there followed a period of stability, but then the town continued to gently expand. A dilemma faced the transport managers: whether to extend the tram network, or to look for different solutions. Already hundreds of the ubiquitous B-type motor bus had been built for service in London and the business that was to become United Counties had been running buses in the county since 1912. Providing additional infrastructure for trams, with all those rails, poles and wires, was expensive. So the first Corporation buses were acquired in 1923, initially operating alongside the trams and in agreement with United Counties, who were already serving the outskirts of Northampton and rural areas. This meant that the Corporation omnibuses were restricted to the town boundaries, working to Abington, Kingsthorpe and St James using five elegant twenty-eight-seat single-deck vehicles with a Thornycroft chassis and Brush bodywork. Thornycroft was an early player in the commercial vehicle market, building petrol-engined vehicles from the turn of the century, and was later known for its specialist fire tenders. Historian John Child recalls that these early buses (Nos 1–12) had solid rubber tyres called 'super resilient', as large pneumatic tyres were not then available. With their crude suspension they must have offered passengers a very lively ride. Initially, the service ran to new housing areas beyond the electrified network, but in reality it spelled the beginning of the end for what was a fairly short-lived tram service. 'The partner became the predator,' as John Child succinctly puts it.

The one big advantage of buses over trams is their ability to go almost anywhere. Trams are also relatively noisy, screeching round corners and grinding along rails. There seems to have been a movement among both the local media and the town council to quickly eliminate the trams and some pressure was put on the General Manager of Corporation Transport, Mr John Cameron. Further buses were soon ordered, including the first vehicles with inflatable tyres, and soon Sunday working was exclusively by buses. Some of these vehicles had bodies by a local firm, York, Ward & Rowlatt, who are still thriving in Wellingborough, these days running car dealerships. Two buses delivered in 1925 had bodies by Charles H. Roe in Leeds and this was a significant, if small, order. The same firm went on to body every new Corporation bus delivered in the 1950s and 1960s.

In 1910, Marefair was one of the busiest parts of town. Here a tram heads towards Black Lion Hill with a carrier's cart heading for town. (John Child Collection)

# Local Body Builders

After the Corporation switched to buying vehicles with a Guy chassis (Nos 13–39), another local firm, W. Grose Ltd, provided some of the bodies. This firm also has a long history as car retailers in the town. Clearly Grose did a good job, for they received eight more orders up to 1930. The later Guy vehicles were beefy double-deck vehicles with six wheels, offering much higher capacity for busy routes, such as that along the Wellingborough Road. The chassis of the Guy vehicles were built in Wolverhampton, and sold very well nationally and internationally. They were the real forerunners of the modern double-decker bus, unlike the old Thornycrofts, which still retained a faint whiff of stage coach. The new fleet of buses, which later encompassed four-wheel vehicles, was so successful that the tram lines were removed in Wellingborough Road by 1930.

From this point, the future of Northampton's trams was in jeopardy. Tram rails and overhead wiring needed regular maintenance, and as more double-decker buses were acquired, the tram network shrank. The new buses delivered in the 1930s came from Thornycroft, Crossley, AEC, Dennis and Guy (Nos 40–66); the types ordered included some powerful-looking single-deck vehicles with front entrances. John Child recalls that re-training former tram crews caused 'severe difficulty' due to the 'skill and brute strength' needed to drive the new buses. There was no power steering or automatic transmission in those days.

The inevitable end for the tram network came in December 1934 when, as is usual with valedictory events, there was a celebratory last run. In the case of Northampton's tram system, however, there really was something to cheer. The town never seemed to love its trams with the passion felt in other places. The rails were quickly removed, although even in the 1960s it was possible to spot the odd roadside pole once used to support overhead cables, and even today the old bus garage at St James still retains tram tracks. When a batch of new Crossley buses (Nos 67–82) was delivered in 1934 to replace the last trams, they were fitted with a type of gearbox that proved so reliable and popular that almost all the remaining front-engined buses delivered to Northampton Corporation were equipped with it. This was a pre-selector gearbox, with which the driver shifted a gear lever to the next ratio and then simply pressed a floor pedal for the actual change to be made. It made for smooth and easy progress for the driver, but by the 1960s – when new Northampton buses still featured it – it was obsolete. Those 1934 Crossley buses, called 'Mancunians', were also Northampton's first diesels, being powered by a huge 9 litre, six-cylinder unit developing about 100 bhp. Eventually there were sixteen in service.

Northampton Corporation Omnibuses' No. 1 was this Thornycroft vehicle with a twenty-eight-seat Brush body. Notice the very elaborate paint scheme and the solid tyres on disc wheels. It is seen here brand new in August 1923; some of these vehicles worked until after the Second World War. (John Child Collection)

These elegant Thornycroft buses came to Northampton in 1924 and had bodywork by locally based York, Ward & Rowlatt. They were Nos 9 and 10 and have a carefully panelled version of the vermilion and white livery. (Courtesy of the *Northampton Chronicle & Echo*)

The Guy FCX typified the six-wheel era, with this robust looking machine being built in 1928. It was fitted with a body by Grose and was the first of nineteen similar vehicles. (David Walmsley Collection)

Here we see a Guy bus, which was delivered in 1927, the location being Kingsthorpe Hollow. The scene is changed beyond recognition today. The car behind the bus looks like a mid-twenties Ford Model T, but the motorcycle combination may be newer, suggesting an early 1930s picture. (John Child Collection)

Two of the six-wheel buses built by Guy in the late 1920s wait to leave Mercers Row. The picture was taken in the early 1930s and shows the well-known Geisha Cafe. No. 32 is on service 2 to Kingsley, while No. 22 is on route 1 to Abington. (Courtesy of the *Northampton Chronicle & Echo*)

A unique bus in the Northampton fleet was No. 40 – an AEC Renown. The fairing above the cab gives a more streamlined look. It worked from 1930 to 1945, and is seen here in Wellingborough Road, near Christchurch, in 1932. (John Child Collection)

A busy scene in front of the Geisha Cafe in Mercers Row, with tram No. 37 having its trolley pole swung round by the conductor using a rope. The driver walks wearily back to the front of the tram. In this year, 1931, the undertaking was renamed Northampton Corporation Transport, but this vehicle still carries the old 'Tramways' name. (Brian Hooper Collection)

Now this is a bus with real presence – what an amazing beast. It is No. 44 (later No. 47), a Guy C single-decker that is seen in George Row in 1931 when nearly new. These racy-looking machines were withdrawn in 1939. (John Child Collection)

Three Crossley Condors were delivered in 1932, with a much more modern look. Many more Crossleys followed up to 1936. No. 41 is seen here at the manufacturers before delivery. Note the intricate lining, which was abandoned after the war. (John Child Collection)

The Dennis Lancet was a popular bus in the early 1930s and Northampton bought seven. This is No. 52, which is seen when new in 1932. Fitted with Grose bodies, these buses survived the Second World War. (John Child Collection)

Crossley No. 66 is seen here at work in Nottingham, before joining the Northampton fleet in 1933. It had been a demonstrator initially registered in Aberdeen. It operated in Northampton until 1947. (John Child Collection)

# Simply Red

After the tram period, the buses were painted vermilion to the top of the lower deck and cream above, including the area around the upstairs rear windows. The roof was red. There was extensive lining to all panels, with the familiar Corporation crest on the bodyside. The words 'Northampton Corporation' were featured in shaded gold between the rows of windows and it gave a very handsome and elegant look to the town's vehicles. The single-deck buses were similar, except that the vermilion finished below the window line with the lettering 'Northampton Corporation Omnibuses' and later 'Northampton Corporation Transport' just below the windows. It presented a very ornate and attractive picture. Destination blinds showed only the service number and final destination.

Business kept growing for the buses in the 1930s as the shoe industry remained strong, and events like the floods in the town of 1939 were nothing more than a hindrance. By 1936, all new vehicles were double-deckers. In that year, a significant trial was carried out between the vehicles of two major UK manufacturers – Daimler of Coventry and Leyland in Lancashire. The Daimler COG5 (No. 84) had a five-cylinder diesel engine and its Leyland competitor, built in large quantities for British and overseas markets, was the Titan TD4. This had an 8.6 litre diesel mated to an automatic transmission. Despite its widespread popularity, the Titan (No. 83) lost out to the Daimler, although both test buses were bought by the Corporation and the Daimler vehicle was a familiar sight on the streets of Northampton until late 1957. York Bros, the local and well-respected coach firm, bought the Leyland Titan in the 1950s and ran it in their fleet for many years.

Having decided to make the Daimler their standard bus, the Corporation ordered twenty-six more over the next three years, the last ones arriving on the brink of war. These had bodywork by Charles H. Roe of Leeds, and this Daimler-Roe combination was to continue in Northampton into the 1960s. The garage at St James was also rebuilt and extended in 1939. It stands to this day, now owned by Church's Shoes, who plan to keep the classic façade as they convert it for a new use.

The 1939 Daimler-Roe vehicles had a teak-framed body (a similar concept to the ash framing in a Morgan sports car). They gave more than twenty years of excellent service, proving reliable and economical. During the Second World War, buses were in short supply, but Northampton received a few new ones. It was a case of taking what you could get and most of those received in Northampton were Daimlers with Duple Utility bodies, numbered 112 to 127. The war saw hardly any bombs falling on the town and it was quickly business as usual after the victory parades.

With hostilities ended, Northampton received twelve more Daimlers with what was basically utility bodywork (128–139). They were immediately followed by ten more Crossleys (Nos 140–149) – the new DD42 model with a very distinctive shrill sound from their 8.2 litre diesel engine. This developed 100 bhp, but that was not much when climbing Bridge Street in a heavy vehicle with a full load. Maybe that is why the Crossleys were usually seen on the flatter routes along the Kettering Road to Broadmead Avenue and Manfield Hospital. The manufacturer quoted 0–30 mph in twenty-four seconds!

Leyland Titan No. 83 was one of two diesel buses used in comparison tests in 1936. This attractive vehicle had an early automatic transmission and, despite coming second to the Daimler, it ran until 1949, when it was sold to York Bros, and remained a familiar sight in the town. (Courtesy of the *Northampton Chronicle & Echo*)

A busy Abington Street scene around 1937. The trams serving the east of the town had gone by 1930 and Guy FCX buses dominated the Kettering and Wellingborough Road routes. (John Child Collection)

Nearing the end of its life with Northampton Corporation Transport is Leyland Titan No. 83. When built in 1936 this metal-framed bus was of a new design, but it lost out to a Daimler in comparative trials. (G. H. F. Atkins, John Child Collection).

The winner of the contest to find a standard bus for Northampton was this Daimler COG5, which became No. 84. It is seen here in 1936 in Far Cotton with some classic advertising on show. The Cobblers' fixtures include West Ham and Southend. (W. J. S. Meredith)

No. 85, seen here in an official photograph, was a Daimler COG5 with English Electric bodywork, and was the first of fifteen such supplied in 1937 and 1938. Some of these plied the streets of the town for twenty years. Thirty years later, Northampton was buying basically the same type of bus. (John Child Collection)

A Utility wartime bus in Utility livery on a damp wartime day; No. 116 is standing next to the old tram shed at Café Square, St James, on its meandering way to Five Bells. This picture was taken in 1944 when No. 116 was just one year old. (The Omnibus Society)

Standing outside the Black Boy Hotel in Wood Hill in 1948 is a Daimler Utility bus with Duple bodywork, No. 126. Northampton ran more than twenty of these at the time and its black radiator grill shows its wartime ancestry. The livery is the attractive post-war style with three bands. No. 129 of this batch still survives. (Courtesy of the *Northampton Chronicle & Echo*)

Careful with the brakes! One of the English Electric-bodied Daimlers, No. 95, cautiously descends Bridge Street in the freezing winter of 1947, with snow piled high by the pavements. Route 19 will take it to Queen Eleanor Cross. (Courtesy of the *Northampton Chronicle & Echo*)

This Leyland Titan was delivered in 1942 when getting buses of any type was difficult. It ended up with York Bros, but is seen here at West Bridge in 1953 looking very smart. The emulsion film of the day has made this vehicle look particularly dark. The three-band paint style was introduced after the war, with each new general manager varying the detail of the vermilion livery. (East Pennine Transport Group)

One of twenty-eight wartime Duple-bodied Daimlers delivered to Northampton between 1943 and 1946 was No. 113, which is seen moving cautiously along Abington Street in 1953 with a sister bus behind. The fashions and buildings repay study. (P. I. Rawlinson)

The end of the war also heralded a new, simplified livery – the familiar vermilion, but with three white stripes and the Corporation coat of arms on the side, but no lettering. In 1947 came the first of the Daimler CVG6 models, the 'G6' denoting a six-cylinder Gardner engine and the 'V' signifying victory over Germany! The first twenty (Nos 150–169) had Northern Coachbuilders bodywork, but from then on Charles H. Roe was the first choice.

By 1951 the town's population had stagnated at around 104,000, of whom 15,500 worked in the shoe industry. As a boy walking to Stimpson Avenue School, I recall the streets smelling of leather and, believe me, there are many worse odours. Barratts, True Form, Manfield and many other volume shoemakers kept the buses of Northampton busy taking an army of 'cobblers' to work and back. Uncomfortable winds were blowing through Northampton and its transport system as the 1960s approached, however. The boot and shoe town found itself facing a crisis as the advent of Charles Clore's 'pile 'em high, sell 'em cheap' British Shoe Corporation led to low-cost imports from Eastern Europe. The highly labour-intensive Northampton shoe industry spiralled into rapid decline and suddenly it was a town searching for a new identity. When Gordon Harmer left the *Chronicle & Echo* newspaper in 1967, his once-coveted role as specialist shoe industry correspondent was found to be no longer needed.

No. 111, a wartime Leyland Titan TD7, is at West Bridge in 1951, two years before it was withdrawn. Notice the half-painted advert. (East Pennine Transport Group)

# On the Buses

Northampton's buses weren't just for passengers; parcels were happily delivered by Northampton Corporation Transport, who ran their own parcels service. In 1939 they would take a hefty parcel weighing 112 lbs (50 kg) anywhere in town for one shilling (5p). By 1964 you could take your package to the Parcels Office in King Street (mornings only on Thursday) where it would be franked with a pre-payment stamp. Or, once stamped, you could give it to a conductor. Collected and delivered, it would cost one shilling (5p) for a 5 lb parcel (2.3 kg) or customers could choose a delivery-only service. United Counties also offered a parcels service and you could go to your local bus station to send or collect a bus parcel. There were endless rules and regulations. For example, Northampton Corporation Transport wisely informed its customers that they could not send bank notes or precious stones by bus.

Buses at this time ran on popular routes every ten minutes from before six in the morning until around eleven at night. The less popular routes, such as number 9, which went to the Five Bells pub in Kingsthorpe via Castle Station and Kingsthorpe Hollow, was half-hourly except at peak times. Today it can be quite fun to hire an old bus for your wedding or another event. Back in the 1960s you could also rent a Corporation bus for your wedding, or 'late dance'. The sign at the front of older buses upstairs saying 'No Spitting' might take the edge off the ambience.

As new buses arrived, old ones headed for the last Five Bells of them all – the breaker's yard. A strange fate befell No. 117 in 1957, which had a double afterlife. It was driven to Duston Mill by Bert Cattell, where the already loosened body was removed to be used as a chicken coop. A team of fitters used jacks to position it on old railway sleepers. Once this procedure had been accomplished, the naked chassis was driven to Cherry Orchard Secondary School for engineering training. No. 205's life came to an end in 1971; it was converted to a mobile office complete with a safe and external doors, where transport staff would book on and off, as their old office had been demolished.

Decorated with a crown to mark the Coronation of Queen Elizabeth II, No. 173 is seen in Mercers Row in June 1953. (P. I. Rawlinson)

A classic Patrick Rawlinson shot of No. 154, now preserved, in its heyday. It is seen on its way back from Weston Favell in Wellingborough Road in 1954. Opening rear windows were an unusual feature of Northampton buses. (P. I. Rawlinson)

A 1955 picture of No. 96, one of ten Daimler COG5s with English Electric bodywork. It is on route 9 from Wood Hill, by this time a home for the more venerable members of the fleet. These buses were built in 1937/38 and were withdrawn by 1957, so they owed their purchasers nothing. (East Pennine Transport Group)

A nice period piece in Broadmead Avenue during 1960. No. 110 is a Daimler-Roe COG5 (the G5 denotes a five-cylinder Gardner engine). This handsome bus retains its wartime black radiator grill and sports the 1950s livery with one narrow white band. It would be fascinating to know what the driver and conductor are discussing – maybe the destination blind? (John Child Collection)

This previously unseen, poor-quality photograph justifies inclusion as the only known colour picture of No. 110, which was taken after 1960 when it was in excellent condition on route 8. Colour pictures of COG5 buses are very rare. It now has a chrome grill. (R. J. F. Rawlinson)

A picture that is full of interest; the Crossley, No. 149, is negotiating the new roundabout in St Peter's Way in 1960, but don't miss the motorcyclist leaning at a jaunty angle with no helmet. The background shows redevelopment taking place following the opening of this road. (T. Tomalin)

A variety of buses in Mercers Row makes a typical summer scene on 7 August 1962. Note that one vehicle carries banners for the Northampton show. (T. Tomalin)

No. 148 leaves the depot at lunchtime on 2 October 1962 to provide a factory special from Midsummer Meadow. These vehicles had Roe bodywork, but a Crossley chassis. (Graham Onley)

Carnival day in Northampton disrupted town centre services. Here on 21 June 1962, a selection of buses is seen temporarily operating out of the Mayorhold. (T. Tomalin)

Conductress Nora Moriarty has a quick conversation with her driver, Denis Casey, before heading to the town centre to join the lunchtime ten-minute service peak on 2 October 1962. (Graham Onley)

Nos 193 and 171, unable to find evening peak time employment on a Friday in July 1962, are parked in the maintenance area of the garage. Office staff member S. J. C. Baxendale is about to enter the body shop for a 'look round' as part of the regular unofficial Friday teatime routine, before heading for home. Office staff were allowed free access to all areas in those pre-Health and Safety days! (Graham Onley)

Still carrying the old narrow-band livery, Northampton bus No. 184 descends Bridge Street on 18 September 1965. Notice the gang of bikers, the little MG Midget and the other period vehicles, including a 'Horrocks for Heating' truck. A 190 series bus follows, about to pass the Angel Hotel.

The peak time service to Military Road was an oddity due to its unique destination blind. Crossley No. 144 is on duty on 27 May 1963 in Abington Square, when the days of this vehicle were numbered. The statue of Charles Bradlaugh, radical MP and secularist, watches over the proceedings. (T. Tomalin)

A line-up for the Omnibus Society, who were visiting later that day, including No. 147 with some 'battle damage' to its roof. The photographer had been 'asked' unofficially to park the buses as a favour for his boss, who was a Society member. The others are Nos 197, 193, 185, 175, 164 and, oddly, No. 151, which had been fitted with a five-cylinder engine. (Graham Onley)

No. 104 and No. 226 in St James' Road during March 1962. Built in 1961, No. 226 was not quite the newest addition to the fleet, but smokey No. 104 was certainly among the oldest, being a COG5 used only for specials. It had been built in 1939 and was in its last months of service. While both buses appearing to be heading for Broadmead Avenue, No. 104's driver was probably still in the process of searching the destination blind for a more appropriate description for the factory special he was about to operate. (Graham Onley)

Graham Onley worked in the office at the bus garage in St James's End during the early 1960s as a general clerk. Among his tasks was reshaping timetables as the Corporation Transport services were in retrenchment. A keen youngster, he soon found himself administering affectionate inspectors old enough to be his grandfather! He recalls it as a very friendly place to work.

'With hindsight, working for Northampton Corporation Transport taught me how to treat people and how to manage,' he says, adding that the buses were almost over-maintained, such was the care lavished on them. The garage was capable of almost anything, including rebuilding a bus body. It would take up to two months to completely overhaul a bus, which included a full repaint inside and out. A team of fine craftsmen worked at the garage, whose skills included woodwork and coachbuilding, which was essential for looking after the Roe bodies' wooden frames. At one stage around sixty garage staff were employed keeping the buses on the road.

One of the new routes in the 1960s was the 6A to Newton Road, which served a couple of large engineering production facilities with hundreds of employees on the west side of the town, Express Lifts and British Timken. Others, like the 18 to Pleydell Road, were abandoned as passenger numbers dwindled. These were troubled times. There were severe staff shortages, especially of drivers who were tempted by jobs with United Counties, Watneys Brewery or working out of town. The transport service was losing passengers to cars and change had to come. The loss of passengers was matched by a downturn in the finances of the transport undertaking, with falling income and rising costs.

A portrait of a Daimler CVG6 of Northampton Corporation Transport – No. 234 is seen in Wood Hill, Northampton, on 18 September 1965. The Midland Bank behind was demolished shortly afterwards.

A view from my bedroom window on 16 September 1965 above the Model Shop in Wellingborough Road. This is something of a period piece, with bus No. 206 approaching on its way to Weston Favell. You can see all kinds of cars, including a 1950s Ford Escort estate, two Morris Minors, a Ford Cortina, Triumph TR3A, Minis, 1100s, a Viva and other transport of the era. Virtually every shop you can see has changed hands ... except for the Model Shop. A United Counties bus is passing St Edmund's Church and the chimney was at St Edmund's Hospital.

This picture was taken in Northampton town centre on 11 March 1966 and shows No. 248 from 1965 in Wood Hill. She was less than a year old at this time. The building site behind is the old Midland Bank.

A lowly job for No. 173 on 18 March 1965. As some of the oldest buses then running, Nos 170–179 were used on the lightly loaded routes 8 and 9 to Five Bells, but also took on more onerous duties.

Freshly repainted and in perfect condition, No. 186 stands at the Manfield Hospital terminus in July 1965. This vehicle was looking very tatty before its overhaul, but here it positively gleams. (P. I. Rawlinson)

No. 186 again, this time hurrying along Wellingborough Road in January 1966.

A familiar view to those who were regular bus travellers in Northampton; the dark red seats with chrome handles were common on all later Northampton buses. A round mirror gives the conductor a view of the platform. This is No. 229, built in 1962, waiting in Mercers Row, Northampton, on 30 January 1966.

Seen in Wood Hill, Northampton, with the Midland Bank being rebuilt behind, is bus No. 244. It was delivered new in 1964. Note Roe's logo beneath the driver's side window. This view was taken on 30 January 1966.

Delivered new in 1962, No. 228 is seen in St George's Avenue on route 14 on a chilly 6 February 1966. The Racecourse is on the right with some classic cars, including a Renault Floride, a Minivan and an old Humber – plus a football match.

*Left*: Daimler No. 175 was built in 1949 and was still giving good service on 5 February 1966. It's seen here at a temporary bus stop before setting off from the town centre to Cotswold Avenue, which was a new route launched in 1960. This view is in the Drapery.

*Below*: In Broadway, Northampton, on 6 February 1966 is No. 223 on route 12 to Dallington. Winter dirt adorns the sides, but normally the town's buses were kept in excellent condition. A big Essex bus washer was installed at the garage at St James, which also looked after many cars and vans of the council, including the Mayor's limousine.

Waiting between duties in Mercers Row, Northampton, is Daimler CVG6 bus No. 162, which is seen on 11 March 1966 after a heavy shower. Note the generally good condition of this vehicle, which was nineteen years old and approaching retirement.

The driver's door hangs open rather precariously on No. 180, which is seen in Wood Hill, Northampton, on 18 March 1966. Burton the tailors is behind, plus an empty space where the Midland Bank once stood. This was the first of the second batch of these vehicles, which had a different waist rail and a one-piece rear window to distinguish them from the 170–179 series.

Off on its way to Dallington with a very light load is No. 181. It has just turned into Wood Hill, with the Market Square behind, on 18 March 1966. The chromed front upstairs opening vent windows have been painted red.

A bit of close parking here from the driver of No. 183 in Wood Hill, Northampton, on 18 March 1966. Built in 1950, these were handsome vehicles and seemed to us (as passengers) to have lively acceleration.

Heading along East Park Parade, Northampton, is No. 213, a Daimler bus delivered in 1959. It looks as though a bit of rudimentary radiator blanking has been added. The cheery side advert says 'Come Co-operative Shopping'. (12 March 1966).

This picture was taken in Wellingborough Road, Northampton, on 11 March 1966. Abington Park is in the background, with a United Counties bus stop. No. 188 was built in 1950 and is out of service – route 9 did not run along Wellingborough Road.

Seen on 11 March 1966 at Weston Favell is No. 225 from 1961, with the Trumpet pub (then a Watneys house) in the background.

Five years separate these two vehicles, Nos 217 and 246. No. 246, later to be preserved, was one of the newest in the fleet at the time, but it is basically the same as the 1960 version in front. Both are in Wellingborough Road on 18 March 1966.

At the time these were the oldest buses in service at Northampton. No. 162 is seen here in Wellingborough Road near Abington Park on 11 March 1966. She was built in 1947 and this type was being taken out of service around this time. There are no passengers and the wrong destination is showing, so she is out of service and the conductor can be seen taking it easy inside.

Standing in Wood Hill is No. 200, the first of sixty-eight almost identical buses supplied by Daimler between 1957 and 1968. This is a nice day in spring, on 18 March 1966. Slight grill styling differences were made on successive vehicles.

Nearly twenty years old and still going strong, this is No. 165 in Wood Hill, Northampton, on 18 March 1966. You can see Oliver Adams, a bakers and coffee shop, on the corner, which had a coffee lounge finished like the inside of an aircraft. No. 165 is in nice condition for an 'oldie'.

Built in 1949, No. 175 is standing in Chiltern Avenue on a grey day, 11 March 1966. These vehicles gave nearly twenty years of excellent service, but sadly none was preserved.

A nice reflection after a shower, starring No. 183. This was taken in Wood Hill on 11 March 1966. Northampton's vermilion paint was a superb colour.

Well loaded, No. 197 passes the old Manfield Shoe factory in Wellingborough Road, Northampton. Part of this is now an Indian restaurant. This picture was taken on 11 March 1966. No. 197 was built in 1953. These were the first 8-foot-wide Northampton buses, previous vehicles having been 6 inches narrower.

On 18 March 1966, Daimler CVG6 No. 229 waits in Mercers Row, Northampton, for its next duty. The small gold emblem over the fleet number was the Roe builder's transfer, another of which appeared on the staircase near the conductor's platform. The narrow white band is the only adornment.

Seen in Mercers Row, Northampton, on route 4 to Broadmead Avenue is 1965 Daimler CVG6 No. 246. This bus had been delivered the previous year and still looks very smart on 11 March 1966. The building on the corner of the Market Square was being rebuilt at this time.

Upstairs, front seat was where we liked to travel. This is a strange view as we seem to be heading for a tree! Note the cream roof, stained by years of smokers, and the notice telling passengers they are not allowed to stand. The bus is No. 225, seen on 11 March 1966.

Still in the old narrow-band livery is Daimler CVG6 No. 232 in Northampton town centre on 18 March 1966. The fleet number under the driver's window varies in position if you examine different buses. On hot days it was normal to drive the vehicle with the sliding door open, alleviating the hot cabs of earlier buses.

A portrait of No. 183, newly repainted, sparkling in Wood Hill in March 1966. The advertisements on the side were painted and, unlike today's movie ads, tended to be there for a long time.

Heading along Wood Hill, Northampton, on 12 May 1966 is Daimler CVG6 No. 186, still looking good after sixteen years pounding the streets of the town. An agreement to purchase this fine vehicle for preservation broke down at the very last minute when the buyer was suddenly informed he had to supply his own wheels. No. 186, sadly, went for scrap.

In the usual nice condition that was a feature of Northampton Corporation Transport vehicles when Mr Dyer was engineer, we have Daimler CVG6 No. 175 standing in Mercers Row, Northampton, on 11 May 1966. It was one of the first of this batch to be repainted in the 'wide-band' livery. 'First in 625' on the advert relates to the higher definition television coming in at the time. Mence Smith's store is behind the bus. One of the girls in the background appears to enjoy having her picture taken.

On 18 December 1966, a row of buses are parked in the garage on a Sunday, ready for the Monday morning rush. From the right they are Nos 172, 182, 237, 246, 185, 203 and others. The older the bus, the more the passenger platform leans down. You can also see slight differences between the 170 and 180 series, such as a single rear upper window and heavier waist rail on the later bus. Just the number plates have been cleaned.

Apart from the removal of the destination blinds, these vehicles look ready for work, but they are actually awaiting their final journey after nearly twenty years' service on the streets of Northampton. No. 163 was the last of this batch to be overhauled and certainly does not look like a scrap vehicle. 18 December 1966.

Just three days old, No. 256 is seen at the Golf House roundabout, Northampton, on 4 December 1966. Can you smell the new paint? In the background is the old Northampton Golf Club.

In Chiltern Avenue, Northampton, on 11 March 1966 is No. 175. This was one of the newer routes, having supplemented the 6 to Bants Lane. The bus has the original chrome ventilators on the front windows, which are painted red on some vehicles.

Introduced to service on 1 December 1966 and seen here three days later in Mercers Row, Northampton, is No. 257. George's Parlour was a very popular town centre coffee shop; Lankester's was a booze store.

Just introduced into service, bus No. 254 is seen in Wood Hill on 4 December 1966. One of those tiny Austin A35 saloons stands against the kerb.

Darkness falls on No. 192, a Daimler CVG6 with Roe bodywork, which is seen just as it is re-entering service after a full overhaul and repaint. The location is the Drapery, Northampton, in November 1966.

Congestion in Wellingborough Road on 16 December 1966, with No. 194 showing its maroon interior. This bus ended up as an open topper in London.

The old enemy in trouble – United Counties No. 681 being rescued in Wellingborough Road when only a year old in July 1966.

On carnival parade days, buses would be parked on the Market Square until the roads were clear for them to go to the bus depot at St James. This shot was taken from the window of the photographers' office at the *Chronicle & Echo* on 15 June 1967. The vehicles are Nos 189, 220, 196, 245 and 248. I borrowed a camera from photographer Pete Allen, who then developed and printed this for me while I waited!

The very fine 1949–50 Daimler-Roe CVG6 models were the backbone of the Northampton fleet throughout the 1950s. Here No. 188 looks to be in excellent condition, but sadly it had fewer than two years left to run. It is seen here in Mercers Row in 1967 with frontal advertising, which was a new innovation. No. 262, waiting to leave for Bush Hill, is brand new. (Roy Marshall)

# All Change

As 1970 arrived, Northampton ran nearly seventy almost identical buses, all of which were Daimler CVG6 double-deckers needing both drivers and conductors. Although the winds of change had been blowing for some years, they missed Northampton Corporation Transport's bus fleet. In the 1950s and '60s, old Daimler CVG6 models were withdrawn, only to be replaced by new versions of the same bus. For the drivers they were different; in fact, each bus had its own individual characteristics, such as a smoother gear change, or better acceleration. The later ones offered more passenger comfort with strip lights, better heaters and a wider body, but you still got on at the back and paid a conductor. By this time nearly all other transport systems were buying one-man buses. At least bus enthusiasts were happy – for them, these were halcyon days.

With the shoe industry in sustained decline, Northampton's destiny, whether planned or otherwise, had switched to light engineering. While the town fathers were – or should have been – contemplating this change, another and even more toxic missile landed on their desks. This was an announcement in 1968 that 80,000 extra people would be arriving over the coming sixteen years as part of London's 'overspill'. At the same time, Northampton, now served by faster electric trains, became a commuter area for London. By 1975, employment in footwear was down to just 3,550, with those mainly being involved in the manufacture of high-end men's shoes like Church's, Crockett & Jones or Trickers. The local football team's nickname 'The Cobblers' evokes the town's history.

Social habits were changing too; a more prosperous population enjoyed personal transport with their cars and bus passenger numbers continued to fall away. Meanwhile, as Northampton's expansion plan was propelled forward, vast new housing areas were built at the east of the town, to be followed by others to the south of Northampton.

To say the development was not handled well is akin to celebrating Dr Beeching as the great saviour of our railways. A headlong rush to cope with expansion created by London overspill was matched by some of the most wanton destruction of fine buildings seen in any Midlands town or city. While the grace was torn out of the town centre, the implications of the expansion plan on an infrastructure already under some pressure were enormous. Where would everyone live and work? How would they move around? This brings us back to Northampton's transport system.

Local government reorganisation in 1974 changed the status of the town and the buses were now titled 'Northampton Transport'. The pressure to economise by introducing one-man buses became irresistible. At last, twenty new Daimler Fleetline single-deck vehicles were ordered (Nos 1–20), entering service in 1973. Somehow they did not find favour and had fairly short lives. Back windows that fell out due to rear engine vibration and pop rivets that corroded quickly were two unwelcome features. There was also a change in maintenance practices, as these and future buses had metal, rather than wooden-framed bodies.

For 'one-man, pay-as-you-enter' driver training, two ex-West Midlands Passenger Transport Executive AEC Swifts were acquired (Nos 21–22) and the CVG6 fleet was gradually decimated as each year saw an increasing number towed away on their last journey. The next new vehicles, starting in 1974, were Leyland Nationals (Nos 23–34) – a ubiquitous design of which more than 7,000 were built, before there was a return to double-deckers. The Nationals proved to be excellent vehicles, being generally well-made and much better than the more stylish Fleetlines.

When double-deckers returned to the fleet, they were Bristol VRTs (Nos 35–70), with the same type of chassis concurrently being bought by United Counties (although with different bodywork). It was possible to travel on essentially the same bus in town and country for a few years. The Alexander bodies on the VRTs were well made and in 1977 and 1978 Northampton acquired thirty-six of them. At the end of the 1960s, the popular services had been reduced in frequency as the transport undertaking tried to gear itself up for a new kind of future. Luckily, they had a man to lead them who was up to the challenge – Chris Mahony.

No. 212 sports a new livery as it navigates St Peter's Way roundabout in July 1972, with white paint around the lower windows. It was eventually decided to paint the white around both upper and lower decks. No. 212, unaltered, was unique. (P. I. Rawlinson)

On 17 August 1972, No. 208, nearing the end of its life in Northampton, heads past Abington Square. The unusual wide grill on these vehicles was like that fitted to a batch supplied for work in Birmingham. This bus became an NCT office. (P. I. Rawlinson)

One of the two ex-West Midlands AEC Swifts bought in 1972 for one-man driver training, No. 22 is seen when new to the town, working route 22 to Acre Lane. Being non-standard, they only lasted until 1977. (Robert Edwards)

In early 1973 most of the older Northampton buses, Nos 200–209, were about to be taken out of service and replaced by new single-deck vehicles. Here we have No. 200 itself in Coppice Drive, Northampton, on 21 January 1973. By this time some of her 'sisters' had already been pensioned off. She went on to become a familiar sight around the town painted dark maroon and serving as a playbus, but was eventually scrapped.

On 20 March 1973 a new Daimler single-decker bus, No. 9, is seen in Bushland Road, Northampton, on route 10. These 'one-man' buses proved very short-lived and all had gone within ten years. I assume many were sold on to other users. They seem to have been quite rarely photographed.

By March 1973, when this picture was taken, the 200 series were among the oldest buses working in Northampton. Here we have No. 202 working out its days on route 8, the 'rest home' for veterans. It is on Kingsley Road and has just passed the elegant White Elephant pub with its distinctive Watneys sign. Who remembers Red Barrel?

Running along Kingsley Road is Northampton bus No. 206. My 1972 Triumph Spitfire is parked and both are very similar in colour. No. 206 is on her way to the town centre via Billing Road on 12 February 1973. For a bus about to be retired it looks in remarkably good condition. It was bought by Leonard and Hubert Foyer from Flore, Northamptonshire. They operated it for a year from September 1973 and sold it to an operator in Wales.

The Fleetlines were followed by several batches of Leyland Nationals, which became the ubiquitous single-deck bus in 1970s Britain. They even formed the basis of many diesel railcars. No. 23 was the first of twelve that entered service in Northampton and looks very smart at the bus garage. (Robert Edwards)

A CVG6 after being fitted with the 'new generation' bus destination blind, No. 262 turns from Abington Street in Wood Hill after route 1 was diverted from Weston Favell to Newton Road. Seventeen buses were modified in this way, including old No. 211 from 1959, to allow compatible working over routes with new vehicles. (John Child)

Newly repainted in 1972 with cream around the windows, No. 213 was the first to be treated in this way and it looked excellent. Later, the cream around the lower front windows was left red. Many CVG6s were withdrawn without being repainted like this. (John Child)

In 1974, Derngate bus station had two years left before services were transferred to Greyfriars. Here Northampton Corporation, Midland Red and United Counties buses are seen in August 1974. (P. I. Rawlinson)

# The Grey Elephant

Part of the modernisation of the town included the construction of a huge new bus station, Greyfriars, which opened in 1976. The good news was that it gave a central point from which all bus services ran. The bad news was, well, everything else, including the absurd office suites up in the roof that remained un-let for most of the building's life. As Northampton expanded confidently east into areas traditionally served by United Counties, there were some heated debates about who should run the extended bus services. In the end, Northampton Transport served most of these areas as they became part of an expanded borough, and there was an uneasy truce.

A more consumer-minded timetable explained the newly introduced twenty-four-hour clock and the phone number of an inspector who would hear your

Opening day, 1 April 1976, at Greyfriars bus station, and seen amid the gloom is No. 265 on route 12. (P. I. Rawlinson)

complaints was listed. But there was no parcels service and no wedding bus hire. For some reason Northampton did not run a service 13 – bad luck, perhaps? With the town's expansion proceeding rapidly, services were reorganised and more routes were introduced. The older destinations, often council-promoted pre-war housing areas, made way for new venues and unfamiliar names.

There was a new sense of momentum for Northampton Transport. By 1981 the service was advertised as 'Go Bus' with a natty brochure listing all the vehicles in the fleet. This totalled eighty-nine, with three old CVG6 buses, Nos 261, 266 and 267, still at work. And yet some of the Daimler Fleetline single-deckers new in 1972, built to replace the old CVG6s, had already been withdrawn. By now there were twenty-eight routes, including, at last, the 13 (no longer unlucky!) to Links View, but some services ran only three times an hour. Happily you could still get to the Five Bells pub – in fact, it enjoyed a much better service. Bus hire was also available again.

Daimler Fleetline No. 19 leaves Greyfriars bus station in the late 1970s on a special working. The one-man buses meant the virtual end of the CVG6 models, only a handful of which remained in service by 1980. (Robert Edwards)

Trouble for Bristol VR No. 42, which has broken down. The ERF rescue vehicle was soon on the scene – it could usually be spotted parked in the bus garage. (P. I. Rawlinson)

In 1981 a batch of Bristol VRTs with East Lancs coachwork was purchased. Here is one of them, No. 72, back in town after having been disposed of to Rosemary Coaches of South Lynn, like Northampton Transport a subsidiary of First. It is seen here in the town centre covering for a shortage of vehicles. (John Child)

Leaving the bus garage is the last CVG6 of all, No. 267, which is ready to work a service to Newton Road in the last years of these vehicles in the early 1980s. It still looks immaculate. (Graham Onley)

Northampton Transport ordered its final batch of six Bristol VRTs with East Lancs bodywork and No. 75 was delivered new in December 1981. It is seen here on private hire in 1986 in another new livery, proclaiming 'Northampton Transport Ltd' ownership. (Robert Edwards)

No. 261 seen at the reconfigured Mere Way/London Road junction on a winter Saturday afternoon in the early 1980s. The destination blind has been changed to match those of the new one-man buses. (Graham Onley)

One of the Bristol VRTs delivered new in 1977, No. 43 is seen here enjoying an afterlife in the Essex area, working for Harris Bus under contract to Transport for London. This vehicle was scrapped in December 1994 and Harris Bus went into administration a few years later. It was one of seven ex-Northampton VRTs that went to Harris Bus, three of which survived to work for other operators. (Robert Edwards)

Northampton Transport's No. 21 was a Bristol LH with Eastern Coach Works body and thirty coach seats. It was one of a pair and is seen here in Lady's Lane on its way to Weston Favell on 19 August 1986. (Michael Dean)

Bristol VRT No. 54 was new in 1978, but it is seen here some years later having acquired the First version of red and cream paintwork. The bus is seen in spotless condition leaving Greyfriars bus station. (John Child)

# The First Bid Wins It

New government thinking in the 1980s brought big changes to the industry. Deregulation of municipal transport services was announced in 1986, leading to their being acquired by private companies. A story in the magazine *Bus Business* in June 1991 showed how much progress had been made in Northampton under its new management. In a story warning about very low profitability among bus operators, Northampton was singled out as the country's most profitable. It made a 19 per cent return, followed by the Scottish-based Grampian Regional Transport (GRT) with 15 per cent. Chris Mahony's appointment in 1974 suddenly looked a very shrewd choice. In 1993 the council sold Northampton Transport to GRT, which in April 1995 became part of FirstGroup when it merged with another private firm, Badgerline. A management buyout was rejected. During the 1990s and 2000s, FirstGroup gradually contracted services in the town, and buses were brought in from other parts of their network – and moved away on occasions. In 2004 the First bus planners decided to try to get creative and dedicated colours to routes – Yellow Line and Orange Line, for example. The whole service was branded 'Over ground'. The frequency varied from every eight minutes to hourly on Sundays.

In an open market, competition was intense – from Stagecoach in particular, with the remnants of what was once United Counties. Country Lion have also prospered. Acquired in 1966 by John Bull, the firm initially operated out of modest premises in Palmerston Road, but have expanded over the years from a minibus operator to a company running luxury coaches, plus school and local services. The Bull family still run the business, which is now a major player in the town's transport.

In the end, the success that FirstGroup enjoyed in other towns was not repeated in Northampton. On 25 July 2013 the *Northampton Chronicle & Echo* announced that First's two remaining routes, 2 and 4 to Rectory Farm and Obelisk Rise respectively, would be withdrawn as First Northampton was 'struggling financially'. It was later reported that all remaining First services would be withdrawn on 14 September 2013. At that time, First had only seventeen buses in Northampton. The company that filled the gap was Stagecoach, ironically still known legally as United Counties, which currently runs the majority of services in town and the county of Northamptonshire as Midland Red (South) Ltd. As Stagecoach is locally based at the former United Counties depot in Northampton, the old enemy finally had control of both town and country bus services. Recently there have been around fifty routes in Northampton, but this is a bit misleading as the timetable includes many out of town services – about thirty were to destinations in the town. The big change in recent years is the sheer number of bus operators. Once it was dominated by the Corporation and United Counties, with a few smaller players. Now there are six or seven operators with a service frequency that varies from every ten minutes to a worrying 'no service' on many routes each Sunday, the bigger players being Stagecoach, Uno (created as a University of Hertfordshire student service) and Country Lion. Services now operate out of North Gate bus station, which opened on 2 March 2014 to replace the unloved Greyfriars building that was appropriately demolished by a controlled explosion. There were few tears. Yet, Northampton lacks the magic touch in building bus stations – North Gate is clearly much too small and now many services are back where they were in the 1960s, starting from the Drapery with travellers standing in the rain. Such is progress!

Although the rate of population growth in Northampton did not quite reach the numbers projected in the heady days of 1968, it has continued to the point where it has passed 210,000, making it one of the biggest towns in Britain, with an employment focus on logistics and finance.

Some Renault-Dodge minibuses with Alexander bodies were added to the fleet in 1987. They were bought in case new competitors created after deregulation arrived using similar vehicles, but were disliked by both operator and passengers alike for being just too small. In early 2017, however, this one was still working in the Blackburn area. (Robert Edwards)

Leyland National No. 30 sports a striking all-over advertising livery as it enters Mercers Row in the summer of 1984. (John Child)

No. 32, seen in Lady's Lane, on its way to Bushland Road on 19 August 1986. The vehicle carries fleet logos beneath the windscreen. (Michael Dean)

Another look at Northampton Transport's contribution to the minibus boom – the eight Renault S56 vehicles numbered 103 to 110. Here No. 104 is about to pass over West Bridge near Northampton station on 14 January 1989, ostensibly heading for Dallington Green ... but looking suspiciously like the staff taxi to the depot. (Michael Dean)

A school special from Guilsborough with Volvo B10 No. 115. John Cotterell is driving in this 1989 view. (John Child)

*Left*: A new Volvo B10M Citybus is about to enter service in 1989 and one of Northampton's maintenance team, John Evans (no relation to the author!), is ready to attach its number plate. Fitted with Alexander bodywork, it later became First No. 38083. (Courtesy of the *Northampton Chronicle & Echo*)

*Below*: Obviously too new to open its doors to let passengers sit on its pristine coach seats, Northampton Transport's Volvo Citybus No. 91 sparkles as it runs along Harborough Road on 9 August 1990. Subsequently named *Knights Templars*, it later moved to the Scottish Borders. (Michael Dean)

A winter's day in 1990, with Bristol VRT No. 63 doing business in Broadmead Avenue. (John Child)

Required to behave like a commercial company, the council-owned Northampton Transport Ltd bought a few coach-seated single-deckers to operate services outside the Borough. No. 112 was a Duple-bodied Volvo and is seen here on Harborough Road working the Guilsborough service on 9 August 1990. (Michael Dean)

The naming of bus No. 100 by Ken Dyer followed Choral Eucharist at All Saints' Church in September 1991. His two passions were combined in one moment. (John Child)

Northampton Transport bought this Volvo B10M single-decker with East Lancs bodywork in March 1992, and it is seen here when fairly new. It was later repainted in First Northampton colours. (John Child)

They weren't always smart! Alexander-bodied Bristol VR No. 62 looks very tatty on 29 July 1992 in Lady's Lane, heading to Headlands. Ken Dyer would not have approved, although shortly before its repaint in 1966, No. 186 looked rather like this. (Michael Dean)

The Drapery, with Northampton Transport's Alexander-bodied Volvo No. 123 dominating the scene on 9 October 1993. Note the name scroll above the destination panel – a number of buses carried locally relevant names at that time. In the background is Stagecoach United Counties Dennis Dart No. 455, one of a batch that spent a very brief time in Northampton. They mainly worked service 80 in a Stagecoach attempt to get a share of the Kingsthorpe traffic. (Michael Dean)

Supported on massive jacks, VR No. 73 undergoes maintenance above the pit at the garage in July 1994. (John Child)

No. 116 was a Volvo demonstrator with a B10B chassis and Alexander Strider bodywork. First registered in January 1994, it is seen here on hire to Northampton Transport in Kingsthorpe Hollow on 11 May 1994 and carrying fleet number 116 on the front in tiny numerals. (Michael Dean)

The penultimate bus to be delivered to Northampton Transport was No. 131, carrying the name *Rose of the Shires* and seen in Lower Mounts on 30 July 1994. No. 131 was a Volvo B10M with an Alexander eighty-two-seat body. Sadly the bus had its upper deck destroyed by fire ten years later and was withdrawn and used for spares. (Michael Dean)

A superb period picture of Volvo Citybus No. 93 *Nene Navigation* passing through Blackthorn on 24 March 1994. One of the new housing areas in the Eastern District of Northampton, Blackthorn looks unusually quiet on this Thursday. (Michael Dean)

In 1993 privatisation arrived, promising a bright future for the town's bus system. One of the first signs of this was a Wright Cityranger-bodied Mercedes, imported from Aberdeen. 'Grampian advances' proclaims the message behind the door (Grampian was the name of that part of FirstGroup when it was a Scottish operation). Here it is seen in Houghton Road on 30 July 1994. (Michael Dean)

This Scania started life in Northampton as No. 341, but later migrated to Scotland, where it worked in Glasgow as No. 61561. It seen here brand new in Northampton in 1997. It became quite common for First to move buses between their operations. (Courtesy of the *Northampton Chronicle & Echo*)

An elegant Bristol VRT, No. 70 enters Greyfriars bus station. Many of these VRTs were sold for further use, but No. 70 broke down in 1999 and was simply scrapped. Its catchy registration ended up on a Northampton bus driver's car. (John Child)

Stagecoach Gold Scania/Alexander Dennis Enviro400 No. 15741 heads for Milton Keynes in London Road on 25 July 2012. The more luxurious buses of Stagecoach Gold connect Peterborough, Northampton and Milton Keynes. (Richard Denny)

Stagecoach Volvo Olympian No. 16698 is diverted along Gloucester Avenue on 21 May 2015 and towers over its surroundings. This was almost the end of the road for these twenty-year-old, Northampton-registered vehicles, and this one was sold in 2016 to a bus dealer in Purfleet for further service. (Richard Denny)

In 2013, Enviro400 No. 15453 was painted in a pseudo United Counties livery to commemorate 100 years of buses in Northampton. Here on 17 January 2014 it finds itself operating the menial 50A Pineham service to Swan Valley business park with no more than a couple of passengers on board. It is almost at its destination. (Richard Denny)

A huge 1990 Country Lion Dennis Condor, built as an export vehicle and then repatriated, provides school transport in Liliput Road, Brackmills, on 10 June 2016. (Richard Denny)

About to leave the Drapery for Towcester is a Country Lion Optare, adding to the variety to be seen in this street. Its departure was enlivened by an idiot 'chicken' cyclist who swerved and circled in front of it as it was leaving. 'Quite normal,' said a lady standing next to me. 9 October 2017.

Stagecoach Alexander Dennis Enviro200 B37F No. 37065 is standing outside Northampton's current bus station with a service to Silverstone (but not to the destinations listed on the side) on 10 August 2017.

Uno Dennis Trident No. 284 is seen at the top of the Drapery, Northampton, on 10 August 2017. Uno Bus Ltd is operated commercially by the University of Hertfordshire, serving students and the public, and has developed routes in Northampton. No. 284 was previously owned by London United and was withdrawn in October 2017.

Passing the APH (Abington Park Hotel) in Wellingborough Road, Northampton, on 10 August 2017 is this 2009 Stagecoach-operated Alexander Dennis B46F, No. 22833, which is heading for Wootton Fields. This is rather different from the destinations proclaimed above the windows, which have yet to be updated. In 2017, eight of these buses were operating out of Northampton.

Brand-new Alexander Dennis Enviro400 MMCs Nos 287, 288, 289 and 290 wait to enter service with Uno in Northampton on 30 September 2017 at Northampton University. The buses will link the University Campus with the town centre and railway station. Versions of this bus can seat up to ninety passengers and options include low bridge warning, satellite navigation and high-back leather seats. (Richard Denny)

Richard Denny captured this Volvo B7TL, operated by Country Lion, returning to the company's depot at Brackmills on 19 September 2017. Better known as a coach operator, this family-run company has a big fleet and operates a number of school contracts each morning in term time. (Richard Denny)

Dennis Dart No. 125 of Uno's fleet is seen here in Horseshoe Street, Northampton on 5 October 2017 ... the days of the local Uno Darts appear to be numbered, this one being sixteen years old. (Richard Denny)

# A Study in Scarlet

Let us wind the clock back. It is the first day of December in 1966 and six new buses are entering service with Northampton Corporation Transport. Every year from 1959 to 1966 the undertaking has purchased half a dozen new vehicles (then five in 1967 and 1968). The attractive bodywork by Charles H. Roe was built at the grandly named Crossgates Carriage Works in Leeds. Daimler and Roe – it sounds as though they would make a splendid combination to construct a royal limousine. So reliable and economical were the Gardner engines that many of them went on to have a further life after being removed from buses, often being exported. Quite a few ended up propelling Chinese junks!

Northampton's passengers still boarded at the rear, but since the late 1950s bus operators had been offered a radical new alternative. Daimler offered a vehicle called the Fleetline with a rear engine and front entrance doors – the same layout as featured on most buses today. But some operators persisted with the old front-engined buses, none more so than Northampton. By then such vehicles, despite their quality and reliability, were an anachronism. Even if the one-man bus was a leap too far, Charles H. Roe had offered for many years a longer version of the CVG6, but with the comfort of front opening doors and more seats.

Back to 1966 and all that. Let's take a ride on that new vehicle. Outside, the vermilion paint gleams. Devoid of advertisements, it has a naked look, with a band of cream above the lower deck to enhance its appearance. A wide chromed motif covers the top of the radiator, representing the 'flutes' found on Daimler cars, and the driver has the luxury of tiny round rear-view mirrors, the one on the nearside to monitor passengers boarding. The compact destination window on the front and rear shows very limited information – just the route number, destination and a couple of intermediate points. Inside is a sea of maroon. The handrails are maroon with chrome fittings; the seats are also maroon vinyl with a chrome frame and there is a big mirror near the top of the stairs so the conductor can view people on the upper deck moving to get off.

Fluorescent lights have replaced the tired, circular yellow bulbs in older vehicles and on the left side is a sign saying that passengers are not allowed to stand. Downstairs we can sit behind the driver and watch him at work (always a him). You can stand in the downstairs area, of course. You never needed to ring the bell. That was part of the job of the conductor, whose metal TIM ticket machine back in the 1950s had a rotary action and a large handle, spewing out flimsy paper tickets with purple writing. (The quickest way to clear a bus, I once discovered as a youngster, was to accidentally lose a white mouse purchased from a stall on the Market Square).

A brand-new vehicle had a wonderful smell, soon to be polluted upstairs by smokers who had opening ventilators above both the side windows and those at the front and rear to clear the air. In a few days this vehicle will look very different, with adverts on the sides for local and national businesses – Permoglaze, Rentaset, Wright Brothers, Hamps Furnishers or 'Drinka Pinta Milka Day'. Those on the back will be for car dealers – Mulliners for Sunbeam, Henlys for Morris. It will then settle down to an unglamorous life of around sixteen years and half a million miles, trundling round the streets of the town. Occasionally – especially in the case of the later buses – it would enjoy a further existence in the hands of another operator, who knew Northampton looked after its buses carefully and that they were a good buy second-hand. Others ended up in all sorts of uses, from a tour bus with the roof chopped off to a mobile play school. A few – a fortunate few – survived to enjoy that most glorious after life, to be preserved by caring enthusiasts ready to lavish the kind of love and attention on them that could never be the case when they were the property of a bus operator.

As an eager junior reporter in the 1960s for the *Northampton Chronicle & Echo* evening newspaper, and initially without a car, my trips to carry out interviews (maybe to see a Golden Wedding couple) often meant going by bus. I soon started to share my enthusiasm for all things involving transport with an unsuspecting readership. I got to

No. 210 is on test after overhaul and repainting and is seen here in Mercers Row, Northampton, on 27 February 1966. The 'wide-band' livery was in use at the time. This is a good photograph for rivet enthusiasts!

know Ken Dyer, who was Deputy Transport Manager for Northampton Corporation Transport, but acted more as Chief Engineer. Ken was a dapper, silver-haired man with enquiring eyes and an enthusiasm for all things mechanical. I suppose today you would call Ken 'media friendly'. He would call to tell me of new developments ('We are trying out a new livery on No. 213; why don't you come down with a photographer and take a look?') And so I did, sometimes also going to his treasure-trove home in the evenings where this strange balance between hobby and career was perpetuated over a cup of coffee. He knew every individual bus intimately and took a great pride in their mechanical and cosmetic condition. A bus just overhauled and repainted looked and felt like a new vehicle.

Kenneth Dyer – manager, engineer and enthusiast. (Courtesy of the *Northampton Chronicle & Echo*)

# Pensioned Off

The day eventually comes when nearly all working vehicles face the trauma of retirement. Northampton buses were no exception. This was the time to head down to St James' End, where a group of old faithfuls would be lurking around the side of the garage, destination blinds removed and ready for what could be their last fateful journey. I say 'could be', because a few went on to live a new life with another operator. This might be as a bus, but sometimes other uses were found. The many unlucky ones would be towed up the M1 to South Yorkshire, where they would be set ablaze and the remains cut up for scrap.

The last four buses of this type, which once numbered twenty vehicles, were withdrawn in December 1966. Here we see Nos 164 and 162, with No. 163 on the left, with a wide-band paint style, and No. 166 next to it. It is Sunday 18 December 1966, a week before Christmas, and surely I should have been doing something more sensible than prowling around the bus garage.

'The bus scrap capital of the UK,' is how Adrian Griffiths, a regular visitor to these yards in Barnsley and Rotherham, described the area. He lives locally and was there to capture the last moments of some Northampton buses in Booth's scrapyard at Rotherham.

Here they stood, silently rubbing shoulders with retired vehicles from all over the country, some piled high on top of each other, while others that actually ran were smashed to pieces through being used to push immobile vehicles around. But in the end they ended up as just so much bent and twisted metal, ready for re-processing.

'You wouldn't believe the number of vehicles they got through,' adds Adrian. 'I got permission from Mr Booth to go round his yard on a Saturday afternoon, always armed with my camera. These places had a smell of their own due to the burning that went on. I know it's macabre, but I really enjoyed wandering around!'

Three former Northampton Daimler buses are seen in the Hoyland storage yard of Hartwood Exports at Barnsley on 18 August 1980. No. 236 has a slightly different livery round the lower front windows. These buses would probably have their Gardner engines removed and then the remains sold to a Barnsley bus breaker for scrap. However, some vehicles were sold for further use. (Adrian Griffiths)

Northampton Corporation Transport's bus No. 218 has reached the very end of the road as it ignominiously awaits its fate in the mud at C. F. Booth's scrapyard at Rotherham on 28 January 1978. It was eighteen years old. (Adrian Griffiths)

Greater Manchester No. 6939 and Northampton Corporation Transport No. 245 on their last legs in the misty atmosphere at C. F. Booth's yard in Rotherham on 21 January 1978. This batch of buses was introduced in 1964 and spent between twelve and fourteen years plying the streets of the town. (Adrian Griffiths)

# The Great Escape

Nobody messed with Joe Hunt. His Romany background meant he was more likely to consult a crystal ball than a Filofax when planning his diary. And he kept tight security on his breaker's yard at Molesworth in Cambridgeshire. The message was clear: 'No Admission'. Mind you, Joe's father, Charles, had been an even tougher customer, allowing a dozen mean Alsatian dogs on long chains to roam around the yard. Like his dogs, Charles Hunt – known to all as 'Bearskin' – did not like enthusiasts. When Joe inherited the business in 1970 he took an equally wary view of all visitors. Enter bus historian John Child waving a crisp £5 note. 'Ah,' said Joe, somewhat surprised. 'This has never happened before. Now *you*, master, are welcome any time.' John became a regular visitor, discovering among the piles of wreckage a small fleet of deteriorating Northampton buses sold for scrap to Joe in the late 1950s and early 1960s.

Joe's yard closed in 1997 and Robin Jenkinson, an enthusiast from Consett in the North East, bought one of those buses that was still basically in one piece – wartime Daimler No. 129. Most of the others ended up as razor blades. In 2000, John went to Consett and bought No. 129, taking advice from two friends from Lincolnshire Vintage Vehicle Society. They confirmed it was restorable as it had a straight body and chassis. The words of his ever-patient wife Carole are not recorded, but probably went something like: 'You ... what?'

'I never thought I would own it,' says John. 'When I bought it I stepped back in time. My wife thought I was crackers! She said, "You will never put that bus right."' And yet it has been immaculately restored to the condition it was in when it was retired from service. The destination blinds were eventually supplied by fellow enthusiast Roy Butler.

'Amazingly,' says John Child, 'he had an attic full of them.' Being delivered in 1945, No. 129 had wartime Utility bodywork by Duple. Its black-painted (rather than chromed) radiator grill and rather severe-looking styling was indicative of austerity, although Northampton Corporation Transport improved them over time with new seats and better ventilation and they gave good service. No. 129 was retired in 1959 and was sold for scrap with three of her sisters to Joe Hunt. It survived on 'death row' for more than thirty years. John spent eleven years restoring it to its present exceptional condition. Just rebuilding the engine took six years. Although it was a huge task, the absence of salt on the Northampton roads in the 1940s and 1950s, plus the high-quality maintenance and paintwork, made No. 129 worthy of restoration.

John says:

> Here is a bus that saw the heyday of public transport in Northampton, the abundance of three bell starts followed by the decline in passenger numbers in the late 1950s. Much evidence of those heady days remained – the worn fabric stair treads, the odd tickets found tucked away, several complete ticket rolls left at the back of the conductor's locker and the last paint date – 5/55.

The restoration of No. 129 was thorough and professional, completed 'in house' in Lincolnshire. When it finally emerged back on the roads in 2010 it brought a lump to the throat of those who had known these buses in their heyday. It was perfection. Since restoration it has covered more than 4,000 miles and is a rare wartime survivor of significant national importance.

No. 129 is not alone. Northampton's No. 146, a 1946 Crossley, was part of a batch withdrawn in the early 1960s to make way for new Daimlers. No. 146 was one of eight sold to Hunt's in 1963 and you can see it standing with several of its sisters in old photos of the yard. This bus was bought by Norman Myers in 1974 and went to Bolton. Norman was passionately keen on it. A 'rescuer' rather like Robin Jenkinson, Norman loved Crossleys and desperately wanted to save a Northampton Crossley from being cut up. He was short of cash, but more than made up for this with his enthusiasm. Norman is known to have driven it as a wreck around Bolton with no insurance and no tax – but it went! No. 146 survived various moves and storage until it ended up in the hands of its present owners, Tony Melia and John Jackson, a few years ago. It was a proud moment in September 2016 when No. 146, fully restored after seven years' work, once more returned to Northampton for the annual Heritage Day.

There are some other remarkable survivors. Among them is No. 154, a Daimler with Northern Coachbuilders bodywork that led a precarious existence until finally being recognised as an important relic. No. 154 was one of a batch of twenty similar vehicles introduced to service in 1947. When withdrawn in 1964, it was good enough to be retained as a bus to train learner drivers. As such it was quite familiar on the streets of Northampton with 'L' plates, but it was pretty much worn out when retired in the early 1970s. No. 154 was then stored at the back of the garage and basically forgotten.

The opening of Northampton's new bus station at Greyfriars in 1974 gave it a new lease of life. Recognised as historically interesting, No. 154 was restored by apprentices so it could be the first bus into the new bus station and used in promotions, but it then returned to its life of slumber. A group of enthusiasts knew of the bus and formed the 154 Preservation Society in 1990, acquiring it and spending £10,000 putting it into top condition. These vehicles were built shortly after the war using unseasoned wood, so many of them had a worrying sag in their bodywork. But No. 154 had been carefully maintained and was still in good condition. One of the biggest expenses in her restoration was the cost of seats – as a learner vehicle, all but one (situated behind the driver and used by the instructor) had been removed. Making a new set was very costly, but with this task complete No. 154 is good for many years' service. Since then she has led a very active life, attending rallies, being seen on heritage runs and once again traversing the streets where she covered more than 600,000 miles in daily service. She is used basically in the summer months, but has made a number of long journeys, one as far as Halifax. On the side is the iconic advert for Adams Bread, recalling a famous Northampton firm that sadly closed down in April 2017 (and who paid for the authentic, classic style, hand-painted adverts).

Having secured No. 154, the same group, recently relaunched as Northampton Transport Heritage, decided to acquire No. 267 – the last pre-selector gearbox bus, the last teak-framed bus to enter service in Britain and one of the last open platform buses to enter service. No. 267 was also one of the last three Daimler CVG6 models to work in Northampton in the early 1980s, retained to work the service to Links View, where the lack of a turning circle meant reversing – and that needed two people to safely turn the bus. Three drivers and conductors were required to operate the route, with all others being in the hands of one-man buses. When all three vehicles were withdrawn in 1984, No. 267 was retained for special duties as by then it was something of a celebrity. It was later acquired by the 154 Preservation Society, who fitted a new engine and put her back to work as an historic bus. It's not unusual to see both No. 154 and No. 267 on the streets where they earned their living. Northampton Transport Heritage have recently acquired 1953 Daimler No. 197 as well. This vehicle was sold to Halls of Hatfield Heath for school work in 1969 and then passed into preservation and attended bus rallies, but it now requires significant mechanical work before it will run again.

Several other Northampton buses have survived into preservation. No. 246 regularly appears in Northampton and is lovingly cared for by its owner, Mike Edmunds. No. 250, having been bought from the corporation by a small consortium in 1981, is at Rushden Transport Museum in a rather poor state; No. 258 is now an immaculate mobile bar for Bowlands Brewery. John Ashmore bought No. 211 when it was retired. He owned the Daimler through the late 1970s and early 1980s after buying it direct from Northampton Corporation Transport. John sold it to a man from Halifax, who carried out an excellent restoration on the vehicle, but it was later passed on to a museum in Germany. It is now believed to be in Slovenia, where it is still running but in a neglected condition. Both No. 246 and No. 267 were in a parade of buses from Greyfriars to the new North Gate bus station on 1 March 2014, prior to the new depot being opened.

Preserved Northampton Daimlers on home ground – CVG6 No. 154 is alongside sister Daimler No. 246 in George Row, Northampton, on 12 September 2011. Under the skin these buses are quite similar, despite the fact that they were built eighteen years apart. (Richard Denny)

John Child's Daimler No. 129 sleeps away in Joe Hunt's scrapyard, with sister No. 136 behind. Both would escape to live new lives. (John Child)

Revival! Painters apply the vermilion hue to bring No. 129 back to life. This was a professional restoration in every way. (John Child)

Refugees from Hunt's yard reunited; John Child's wonderful wartime Daimler No. 129, restored to pristine condition with the correct adverts on the side, is seen in Northampton with Crossley No. 146. (John Child Collection)

A new life for a Northampton CVG6 – still resplendent in its immaculate Northampton livery, No. 258 has been converted to the Bowland Brewery bus bar. It is seen here at the Great British Food Festival at Stonyhurst in Lancashire in April 2017. (Paul Brookfield, www.flickr.com/photos/lancashire)

On 8 September 2012 there was a 'great gathering' of preserved Northampton buses, with No. 129 passing Nos 154 and 246 in George Row. Just like old times! (Bob Mullins)

In June 2016 at Warmingford, restored No. 146 stands alongside the remains of sister No. 141, saved for spares. Both came from Joe Hunt's yard. (John Child)

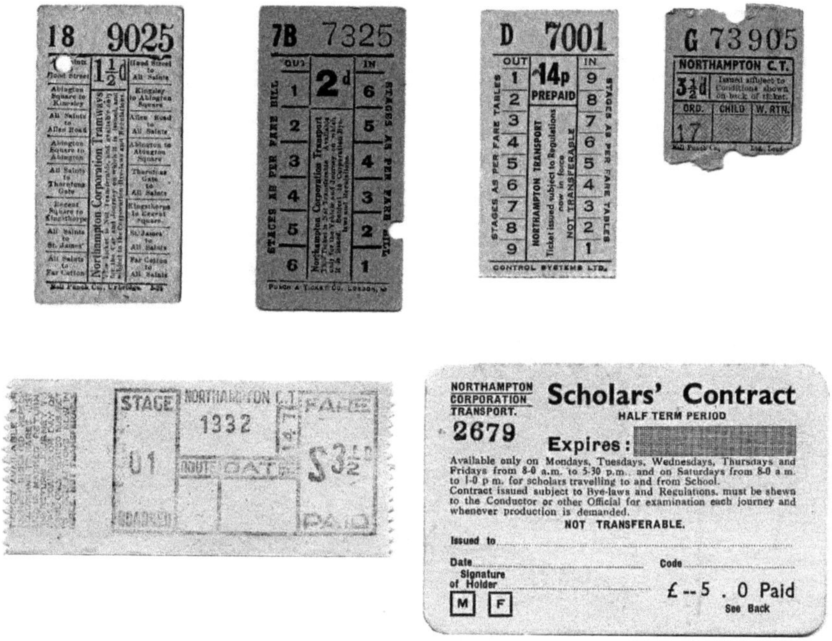


A sample of Northampton old bus tickets in the care of collector Geoff Budd – they form part of the town's social history. From top left to bottom right they are: a 1924 train ticket; a 1934 bus ticket; a prepaid ticket; an Ultimate from the 1950s onwards; a TIM used until the 1950s; and a 1950s school pass. (Geoff Budd).

Two old tram waiting shelters survive. This one is by the White Elephant at the Racecourse and the other is near the Cock Hotel. (Nick Evans)

# Bibliography

Barty-King, H., *Expanding Northampton* (London: Secker & Warburg, 1985).
Brown, C., *Northampton 1835–1985 Shoe Town* (Chichester: Phillimore & Co., 1990).
Child, J. C., *British Bus Systems Number Five, Northampton* (Glossop: Transport Publishing Company, 1985).
Lane, K., *Glory Days, United Counties* (Hersham: Ian Allan Publishing, 2005).
Pinder, M., *Bus & Coach Datsfile No. 13 – Preserved Buses and Coaches 2012* (Hartlepool: HB Publications, 2012).

*First Electric Tram in Far Cotton* (Far Cotton History Group).
*Northampton Corporation Transport Official Timetable* (Northampton: Northampton Corporation Transport, various issues).
*Northampton Mercury* and the *Northampton Chronicle & Echo* (various issues).
*United Counties Fleet Record and Company History* (Northampton: United Counties, 1964).

http://cottonites.co.uk/transport.htm – Transport in Far Cotton (accessed 4 October 2017).
www.mikesbuspages.com – Mike's Bus Pages (accessed 28 September 2016).

Northampton Transport Heritage has recently been established to take on the continued preservation of former Northampton Transport buses Nos 154, 197 and 267. Their wider remit is to cover public transport throughout Northamptonshire and they can be contacted at NTHmembership@outlook.com.